How Long Has This Been Me?

How Long Has This Been Me?

Poems

DALLAS M. LEE

RESOURCE *Publications* · Eugene, Oregon

HOW LONG HAS THIS BEEN ME?
Poems

Copyright © 2025 Dallas M. Lee. All rights reserved. Except for brief quotations in critical publications or reviews, no part of this book may be reproduced in any manner without prior written permission from the publisher. Write: Permissions, Wipf and Stock Publishers, 199 W. 8th Ave., Suite 3, Eugene, OR 97401.

Resource Publications
An Imprint of Wipf and Stock Publishers
199 W. 8th Ave., Suite 3
Eugene, OR 97401

www.wipfandstock.com

PAPERBACK ISBN: 979-8-3852-5814-7
HARDCOVER ISBN: 979-8-3852-5815-4
EBOOK ISBN: 979-8-3852-5816-1
VERSION NUMBER 08/15/25

For Mary Carol, always

*Instructions for living a life. Pay attention.
Be astonished. Tell about it.*

—MARY OLIVER

Contents

About the Author | ix
Acknowledgements | x

Photographic Memory | 1
How Long Has This Been Me? | 2
Standpipe Mountain 1942 | 3
As a Newborn Baby Brother of Three Girls | 4
No Pants | 5
Eye on the Sparrow | 6
Milky Way Band | 7
Walking on the Ceiling | 8
Save the Bones of First Baptist | 9
Young Prodigals | 10
Boys Forever | 11
Best-Ever Cub Scout Project | 12
Texas Sword Drill, 1952 | 13
Small Remains | 14
Monkey Wrench | 15
Winging in as if From the Old Testament | 16
Books of Paper and Ink? | 17
Arranging Our Bookshelf as if for a TV Interview | 18
Long Ago Friends | 19
Tornado | 20
Certitude | 21
How Do We Not Imagine? | 22
The Divide | 23
Moon Jelly | 24
Grand Central Station | 25
Sands of Time | 26

Lonesome Dead Letter Bin Blues | 27
The Pear Tree | 28
Baseball in Black & White | 29
Perfect Pitch | 30
Freshman 1961 | 31
Happy Hour Mayhem | 32
Dear Elvis in Heaven | 33
Ben's New Dictionary | 34
Like A Child | 35
That War! | 36
The Gift of Darkness | 37
Big Bang | 38
Poverty | 39
From that Montana Bluff | 40
The Sunflower | 41
Tiny Seashells | 42
After Hours in the Gallery of Poems | 43
That Deacon's Joke Still Thrills Me | 44
Life's Sweetest Mystery | 45
Benediction | 46

Notes | 47

About the Author

Dallas Lee is a retired journalist/speechwriter and author of three books—*The Cotton Patch Evidence* (Harper & Row 1971), which chronicles the pre-Civil Rights-era experiment in Christian communal living called Koinonia Farm, where the initiative to build quality affordable homes evolved into Habitat for Humanity; *The Substance of Faith* (Association Press 1972), edited from tape-recorded extemporaneous presentations by Koinonia founder Clarence Jordan, who earned a college degree in agriculture and a doctorate in New Testament Greek; and a book of poetry, *No Kind of Blues* (Archway 2022). Lee is a native of Graham, Texas and a 1964 graduate of Baylor University, and he lives in Charlotte, North Carolina, with his wife, Mary Carol.

Acknowledgements

Grateful acknowledgment is made to the editors of the following journals who first published versions of these poems:

Photographic Memory—Avalon Literary Review
Arranging Our Bookshelf as if for a TV Interview—Panoplyzine
The Pear Tree—Panoplyzine
Perfect Pitch—Sport Literate
Against All Odds—Stardust Review
Moon Jelly—Sequoia Speaks
Ben's New Dictionary—Connotations Press; also, an earlier version appears in a book of poetry titled *No Kind of Blues* by Dallas Lee.
Texas Sword Drill—earlier version also appears in *No Kind of Blues*.

Photographic Memory

How I wish I could find
that old black & white
photograph—the six of us
seated around our narrow
kitchen table, small glasses
of prune juice in front
of plates with fried eggs
and the smell of coffee,
holding hands while dad
says the prayer . . . except—
how could this be true?
Only dad knew how to use
that big black square
Speed Graphic camera?

How Long Has This Been Me?

I exit in low gear with a diagnosis
so matter-of-factly delivered that
I'm likely to forget it, so I pause
to jot it down on a bookmark before
I disappear into the parking deck—

>   *Mild cognitive impairment,*
>   *nothing pathological.*

I think of that day in third grade when
I walked home at recess as if the final
bell had rung. Walked right past empty
busses and full playground. Shocked
my mom, who rushed me back in the car
and came in to explain to Miss Kinney
in front of classmates too awed to laugh.

My mother, who so often teased—
>   *You remind me of the man*
>   *who jumped on his horse*
>   *and rode off in all directions—*

a line gathered from her own reading
and, I've come to believe, a mirror
of her own echoic reveries.

Driving home, I click on a favorite CD—
Harry Chapin, *Let Time Go Lightly*—
anticipate how my wife will laugh,
kiss me, declare—*Finally! A name for it!*

Standpipe Mountain 1942

Were it truly a mountain I'd say
I was born in its shade, but merely
a hill with a big round silvered
water tank once blackened against
the threat of Japanese or German
planes getting as far as North Texas
to bomb Graham's town square
and its three movie theaters, library,
shoe shop, bakery, drugstore, feedstore
and classic old courthouse—maybe
even First Methodist and First Baptist
in their nearby catty-cornered standoff.

As a Newborn Baby Brother of Three Girls

words rushed in with my first breath—
whispered, shouted, sung. A merry mix
of talk and tunes—*Don't Fence Me In,
Amazing Grace, Boogie-Woogie Bugle Boy*,
music dancing and sparking my mind
to marvel at this bright world. Mother's
hair on my ears and kisses on my cheeks,
papa's blue eyes and kind hands. Now—
here I am, a father, uncle and grandfather
who forever regrets how hard I argued,
persuading my father to let me stop piano
lessons so I'd have more time to play
hide-and-seek and baseball—and climb all
the trees on Third Street yards and alleys.

No Pants

In memory of Lina Ruth

For me—youngest
and smallest of four kids—
our home was as safe as
I imagined heaven to be
until one bedtime in my
fourth year came a first
stab of anxiety. I slipped
down the hall to where
everyone else was talking
and whispered to mother—
>*What if I wake up as tall*
>*as everybody? I've*
>*got no pants that'll fit.*

She smiled and reassured me,
so I shuffled back to bed.
Then I heard *laughter*—
she had told! I pulled covers
over my head until . . . *footsteps!*
My oldest sister, who never
teased or cuddled, marched
in and hung a pair of *her* jeans
on a nail in *my* closet, left
without a word. I fell
right to sleep, wondering.

Eye on the Sparrow

Growing up in north Texas
any bird I could not name
was a sparrow to me.

The only exception I recall
is the mockingbird that woke
me every morning singing

preacher-preacher!—or so
my mother declared. Yet it was
always sparrows that perched

in my heart, even as I shot them
with my BB gun, buried them
beneath the willow, marked

each spot with a stone, prayed
the one hymn I knew by heart—

*His eye is on the sparrow
and I know he watches me.*

Milky Way Band

As a boy, I often daydreamed
I led a band called Milky Way—
Me at the keyboard, Snickers
on drums, Mars Bar on fiddle,
vocalist a female called Mounds
of course, and shame on me!
But excuse me, too. Coconut
smothered in chocolate was
a mouth-watering first love,
back when I was just a little
finger-licker trying to imagine
how it would be to be a man.

Walking on the Ceiling

Flat on my back where my dad's
slap landed me, I stared at our kitchen
ceiling—a familiar sight. I often
strolled through the house looking
down into mother's hand mirror,
a game my sister Grace and I called
walking on the ceiling! 'Tho only six,
I knew I was wrong to shine my
army flashlight into dad's darkroom
trays, knew he swung at my light,
not me. I welcomed his strong arms
quickly lifting me as I stared at his
darkroom safelight—a soft glow
as forgiving as moonlight.

Save the Bones of First Baptist

For sale—1907 House of Worship

Cathedrals and Temples are built to last
    and often hallowed with saintly remains.
Generations come and go, the flavor lasts.

Believers of protestant persuasion often
    think like sports franchises and tear down
to rebuild with larger skyboxes—or they

sell to build bigger elsewhere, which is
    how this treasure comes to market.
What to do with it? Well, save the bones

for soup, mama said. How about a five-star
    restaurant and pub? Art museum? Theatre?
Why not a country music or blues venue?

It's seasoned to the rafters with song, prayer,
    lust—every strain of the human stain.
Stirs melodious dreams of boyhood church

and my first taste of passion, staring down
    from a curvaceous balcony at Miss Womack
in the choir loft—that River Jordan painting

above the baptistry a perfect roots note,
    Miss Womack a fine Patsy Cline.

Young Prodigals

We climbed the sycamores that
lined the lawn of First Baptist
and tried to imagine those boys

in the Bible. Didn't Daniel
fear the lions? Jonah the Whale?
David that giant Goliath?

Those guys in Nebuchadnezzar's
fiery furnace tested our imaginations
the most. Surely that was hell.

But the lad who worried us most
was Isaac, shown in our Bibles
tied up like a goat with his dad's

knife at his throat! Saved by an angel,
but we wondered why on earth did
Isaac not break free and run for his life?

The father we loved best rushed
with open arms to welcome a son
stumbling home full of shame.

Boys Forever

We wondered and declared
our guesses to huge questions—
How far is forever? Easy—
it's how deep we see into night
skies when the moon is full.
At church, we often heard about
the eternal but never spoke of it—
until we discovered a book
of art in the First Baptist library.
There we found a full-page display
of a young woman—full frontal naked—
hoisting an empty wine glass,
and on that page the word Eternal!
Whenever the coast was clear
we returned again and again,
rushed away with cheeks a'blush,
certain we had seen our own
forever on that glossy page.

Best-Ever Cub Scout Project

We built that teepee
by draping feedstore bags
over long skinny limbs
tied at the peak with leather
strips we'd saved for lanyards.
We staked it taut and high
as a ceiling, then rampaged
through yards and alleys
yelping as fiercely as soprano
boys were able, waving our
dime-store bows & arrows—
until came the evening we lit
a twig fire. Didn't Indians cook
inside teepees? Instantly it
whooshed aflame and I ran
for the hose, desperate to keep
parents unaware. Jacky flung
fistfuls of dirt. But my sister
Grace shrieked *Daddy!* and oh
Lord, here he came! To this day
I hear the screen door slamming
behind him as he seized that
hose from my hands, doused
the flames, sprayed the garage
roof and nearby picket fence,
spun as if to scold, and with
tears in his eyes said—
    Are you kids OK?

Texas Sword Drill, 1952

Ten boys, 10 years old, King James Bibles
at our sides, stand at attention for the command—
Draw swords! then swing those good books belly high
for next orders—*Deuteronomy chapter one, charge!*

Thin pages riffle 'til I get there—Beat Hugh,
our brightest and quickest—and read aloud,
These be the words which Moses spake . . . .

We fly through a lot of *spakes, thees and thines*
learning to navigate scripture before we land
on the story of David, that boy who *slew*—how we
love that word!—who slew Goliath with a slingshot,
then sawed off that giant head. Thrilling, but . . .

Hugh raises a question he cannot finish—
*Is a slingshot same as a . . . same as what we use
to scatter birds? To bomb each other with pecans
and chinaberries? To break bottles in the alley?*
    Same as, uh, as uh . . .

I snatch the words from Hugh and spit them out—
    Same as a nigger-shooter?

    Silence.

With no friend or even acquaintance of color
we have blundered into revelation. If not hate,
hate's spittle has flown with our every flung stone.

---

* 1915—"*Nigger-shooter* . . . sling shot, composed of a wooden handle
with forked limbs and two rubber bands ending in a leather 'pocket' from
which stones are shot. Every boy in Texas is proficient in its use." (Dictionary of American Regional English, UW-Madison.)

Small Remains

Memories of our father

Battered gold wedding band. Sweat-clogged
50th anniversary watch. Exhausted wallet.
Pocketknife so faithfully honed a third of its blade
was sacrificed to a ceaseless ritual of sculpting
his perfect quarter-moon fingernails. Odd, how
tailored-clean were hands worn thick with labor—
making, fixing, digging, planting—yet as delicate
with the silky pages of Bibles and study books as
they were forceful with tools and fix-it challenges
that tested him near to cursing. Like the time
he wrenched the clutch from my Cushman scooter,
or strained atop a ladder to mount that backboard
on the garage. And he no mechanic or carpenter
but small-town pastor with listening ears and heart,
his concentration at study so severe I'd have
as soon stuck a nail in a socket as to interrupt him.
But when he focused, his tenderness was fierce
as his grip. Our town knew in those post-war years.
Young men knocking at the parsonage. Phone
ringing late. Accidents. Illness. Death. Now, we
share books with spines bearing his Dewey Decimal
hieroglyphics, his polished cut stones and stained-
glass manger scenes. Somewhere to be rediscovered
await his wedding band, watch, wallet. Our attic?

Monkey Wrench

Patience was plentiful
in our little frame house.
I just never could find it
in my dad's toolbox.

Winging in as if From the Old Testament

"... they sense at once that here is a landing in the geologic past."
—Sand County Almanac

Thirteen pelicans in an undulating V
bank steeply into Jupiter Inlet, descend
in formation without further wing strokes
and skim waves for a hundred yards before

flaring into soft touchdowns on the tide-
peaked Loxahatchee—*River of Turtles*
in the Seminole language. We lower books
and watch them re-launch, circle, dive

for fish, splash like cannonballs, then
float at ease. A gull lands on one's head
and remains like a neighbor stopping by
to gossip. Soon the big birds re-organize

facing shore, thrash wings to shoo schools
of tiny herring into the shallows, then dive
to swallow them whole. We recall that Moses
listed pelicans among the unclean, but soon

the belief emerged that pelicans perform
a Christ-like blood sacrifice when they
regurgitate hash into mouths of newborns—
such reverence lasting until pelican feathers

were declared ideal for women's hat plumage,
then—*BANG!* An age of mass slaughter began.

Books of Paper and Ink?

All dead or dying. Dostoevsky?
Buck or best offer in yard sales.
Ditto Shakespeare, Milton, Dickens,
Blake, et al. All their pages in Earth's
65,900 languages would not fill a thimble
on the World Wide Web. Cervantes?
Same, maybe sadder—he's funny!
Melville? Google whales. O'Connor?
Go online, read the Bible for yourself.
Yeats, Bishop, Lowell, Milosz, Kunitz,
Oliver, Lux? Mere poets, their words
damned to landfills where worms
consume it all, blind to the light.

Arranging Our Bookshelf as if for a TV Interview

I keep trying to read the titles
—Jeannette Cooperman, The Common Reader

The Poisonwood Bible
My word, Barbara Kingsolver, what sparked
this? *Maybe I'll confess the truth, that I rode in
with the horsemen and beheld the apocalypse,
but I was only a captive witness.*
Anna Karenina
Such passion your words arouse, Leo Tolstoy!
*Those reveries that filled her imagination . . .
something joyful, burning and exciting.*
Silence of the Lambs
Thomas Harris! Did Southern Baptists jolt you
into imagining a monster *no more bound by fear
or kindness than Milton's were by physics?*
Breathing Lessons
What sweet ache of yearning, Anne Tyler!
*I'm so tired of dating . . . I want to sit on
the couch with a regular normal husband
and watch TV for a thousand years.*
The Grapes of Wrath
Amen, John Steinbeck! *The sinners is awful strong
around' about. Wicket people, wicket going's-on
a lamb'-blood Christian jes can't hardly stan'.*
Lonesome Dove
Lord a'mighty, Larry McMurtry! *It ain't dying
I'm talking about, it's living. I doubt it matters
where you die, but it matters where you live.*
A Man Without a Country
Thank you Kurt Vonnegut, for daring us—
*Practicing an art, no matter how well or badly,
is a way to make your soul grow. . . Sing in
the shower. Dance to the radio. Tell stories.
You will have created something.*

*Italicized lines are direct quotes from the texts.

Long Ago Friends

Got a call the other day from the daughter
of a long-ago friend. My first thought—
Sarge has died! But no, she said, he remembers
me and wishes I would call. Wonderful!
All these years and he too thinks of our cub scout
meetings at the parsonage, our happy wasted
days in flat ole north Texas. So, I call and she puts
Sarge on the line. He has little to say, so I chatter
away, wondering what's become of Darrell,
Jacky, David and Joe. *I don't remember them*,
he says. I rattle on about ball games on the lawn
of First Baptist, and did he recall the kind old
janitor Mr. Crawford rising from the basement
to watch us? Or that time Joe McGee leaped
from behind the cedar shrub loudly singing
Mona Lisa-Mona Lisa with skinny arms raised
theatrically, a priceless stone in my streambed
of memories. *No, I don't remember that.*
At a loss, I simply say—God bless you,
Sarge, thanks for tracking me down.

Tornado

The kewrossity of it
says the gaunt man over
and over, ignoring the AP
reporter following along as he
circles his small frame home,
now sitting cattywampus
30 feet southeast of its
footings—cellar exposed
to still-volatile sky, roof
and windows long gone, yet
right next to the fireplace
in that far-flown living room
stands a vase with a dozen
sunflowers, undisturbed.

Certitude

We sinners yearn for it and often
declare it. When my tongue swells
with insist-insist, mornings come hanging
with a laundry line of embarrassments.

Dogma lies ugly in last night's punch bowl.

Maybe it's not a party. Maybe it's on
a sidewalk after church, in a bar in front
of three ball games, stentorian in some
chamber rousing troops or voters.

Repent! my inner-voice soon commands.

And I do. I return to faith and my little
valve of doubt for blowing off the steam
of always knowing. Better a wetted
finger aloft. Even faith needs to know

which way a fresh wind blows.

How Do We Not Imagine?

Trillions of stars
endless light years
from biblical Earth—
how do we *not*
imagine countless
creation stories?

The Divide

A memory of the Palm Beach Poetry Festival

A lime-dotted butterfly butts
the poetry class window as if
desperate to escape, so I rise
and trap it in my palms, step into
the hall, shoulder open a door
and set it free, only to see it
swoop onto an outside pane
and resume tap-tapping, as if
investigating what divides
all it sees from what it feels.

Moon Jelly

for Mary Carol

I fall right away for winks of blue in nature.
Mexican primrose, forget-me-not, bluebonnet . . .
each a gem but not the shade sought, so on I go,
certain nature hoards a tone my lover's eyes attain—
a breathing color, not cold beauty of stone,
though I love how lapis lazuli trills my tongue.

Many eyes yearn toward what I seek to name—
the jackdaw's stare, the koala's touch-me-nows,
gleam of grackle, spider monkey, lemur, bush frog,
barn or barred owl, dragonfly in Gunung Palung,
dwarf bunnies in the low country, sled dogs in
the Arctic. Robins, starlings, satin bower birds,
a wall-eyed buckskin colt for sale in Kentucky,
a shih tzu stud with a business card: "*Bud—Call Me.*"

On and on until the obvious stirs me—the ocean's
eternal motion, absorbing every light that strikes,
where all is pigment, as Matisse and Monet said
of the world. I dive. Predator eyes of some sharks?
Not bad. A vampire squid's blue shields, a humpback
whale's flashing irises while singing, the cornflower
wink of the dolphin fish, then . . .

Yes! Rousing into view is a creature sporting visual cues
I crave—the moon jelly, a medusa of willowy here-I-am
translucence. I reach to touch a beauty that devours . . .
and lurch awake, still at water's edge. Jupiter inlet
is yielding, the ocean plume swelling in, and there—
not the exotic, the new, but the near, the familiar,
the laughter-aroused hue of my lover's eyes.

Grand Central Station

Drunk on celebration, we stepped in
for warmth, leaned over that great
chamber and looked down on a thousand
hearts pounding in all directions into
winter's joy and season's fate while we
huddled above, aglow with the light of our
10th or 12th or was it 16th honeymoon?
How flush with wonder we were, thriving
in that second-chance era of our lives,
a warm room only three blocks away with
a big bed against a tall window overlooking
acres of windows glistening like stars.

Sands of Time

Is one day better
than the other when
every day our eyes
meet is a gift? When
from the start we
knew we would be
friends? Sifting
our beginnings
is like dancing in
the origins of wind.

Lonesome Dead Letter Bin Blues

That love letter
if ever she wrote it
never arrived

If ever her tears
damped a page for you
you never got it

If ever her tongue
sealed and stamped one
her legs—*those legs*—

never sashayed down
the walk to post it

If ever she thought
she would she never—

Can you accept it?

No? Then mail her
a bushel of verbs
sealed with a tease—

Write 'til you blush
and return to sender.
    Please!

The Pear Tree

An "E-poem"
—a type of visual poem created by E.E. Cummings

Far from home on assignments I often walk early and stand
before trees, ponder the fullness
of crowns lifted as if in praise
and alive with unseen choirs—
ee-oh-lay of wood thrush, *shrill*
of wren, *whistle* of oriole, *baritone*
hoot of owl—melodies of joy in a
world of mutual fate. Eight decades gone now and I remain
that boy who climbed the thorny
mesquite tree to honor its presence
before hurrying for a higher climb
in our pear tree, where I imagined
adventures, watched sisters come
and go, spied on passing cars, picked
low hanging fruit and relished the unwashed truth of nature.

Baseball in Black & White

Dad! Let's throw, catch, hit, chatter!
I'll grab our bat, ball and gloves and you
can show me again how fast Stan Musial
uncoiled to hit inside fastballs. How that tall
pitcher Ryan Duren was so blind teammates
had to aim him at the catcher. No time?
OK, I'll pitch a tennis ball against the chimney,
field it and peg it so hard it bounces back hot
and I scoop it like the Orioles' Brooks Robinson.
I'll remember how when you were a boy you
played ball alone when no brothers or playmates
were around. How you'd hit a ball sky high,
run to catch it, then throw so hard and run
so fast you were sliding into home when
the ball arrived and you tagged yourself out,
back when Texas had all the stars in the world.

Perfect Pitch

At the peak of his windup
Roy Halladay stared at his toes.
Fernando Valenzuela looked
up so sharply his eyeballs rolled
into his head. Ryne Duren was tall,
thick, threw fearfully hard, but
what batters feared most were his
headlight-thick eyeglasses and how
he'd lean and squint to locate
the catcher and read the pitch sign—
fastball in, fastball low, fastball up
and away. Best pitcher for boys
to emulate, 'tho? Adam Wainwright.
He has such perfect pitch, players
ask him to sing at their weddings.

Freshman 1961

In memory of Nick Vaughan

Summer classes done, I stand at the stove
staring at still water, fist of salt raised
for boxed macaroni & cheese. Time slows

to its pace in grade school, when I'd watch
the long red wand *tick* toward the recess bell.
After a wee eternity, the air signals that

my brother-in-law Nick the math professor
is passing behind me, so I say—*if I keep
staring at it, this water will never boil.*

Six decades later, still I see the balloon
of Nick's reply trailing his bald head into
the dining room like a cartoon bubble—

>   . . . *Of course it will.*

Happy Hour Mayhem

In memory of Jeffrey Donnell

In that happy hour, we had no clue
of the tumor massing in your brain,
that your final days drew near.

Martini high and laughing out loud,
we scrambled over bookshelves
and rifled through novels we hoped

would satisfy our thirst for a phrase
that would add spice to an old draft poem
like a splash of salt in beggar's soup.

I reached for Don Quixote, quoted
Sancho Panza—*Each of us is as God
made him, and often much worse*—

but gained only scornful eyerolls. You
reached for your favorite—Middlemarch.
We hooted, so you reached again.

Then we smiled—Madame Bovary!
You thumbed to a page and read aloud—

*Love, she believed, must come
suddenly, with thunder and lightning.*

We laughed and raised our glasses.
Only a memory now, eternal as the tides.

Dear Elvis in Heaven

When you wrote, what inspired you—
    a nudge in heart or loins?

A yearning for your own beguine?
    Some lithesome skirt of piety
in your dreams? I write because
    I just read a vow that does not

reveal to whom it is addressed—
    *. . . to go on loving her until
    in the end she loves me too.*
Wow. Sounds like you—but no!

Vincent Van Gogh wrote that about
    a woman whose *never, no, never*
haunted him evermore, perhaps even
    now in Paradise. If you see him, ask.

Vincent might recite these lines—
    *The more she disappears
    the more she appears . . . .*
Oh, how I wish I had written that.

I pray daily that absence of envy
    is a blessing in Heaven. Surely
    you know by now, so please!
If possible, answer by return mail.

Ben's New Dictionary

*for our young friends Ben and Lindsey Poole
and our grandsons Dallas & Dillon Lee*

Ben's new dictionary is so heavy
I said it must have a lot of big words in it
but Lindsey said words don't weigh anything.
Hmm. Toss a handful of words down the well,
which splashes first—thunderclap, yellow or red?
From the trip's backseat when he was 4, grandson
Dillon said, *What if my head was as big as China?*
His 6-year-old brother Dallas replied:
 For one thing we wouldn't be riding in this car, stupid!
With or without irony? Exactly.
Moments later, playing with the latch, Dallas asked,
 Why does the word lock have a 'c' in it?

Smart question was the best I could do. Then I rallied:
Words do play, I said. Take the S's. Slip: slip knot,
slip down, slip you a dollar, boat slip, "slip-slide away...."
Step: stepladder, step along, big step in life, stepfather.
Still: hold still, whisky still, "Still crazy after all these years...
 Simon. Paul Simon, Simon please...."
Steal: steal a pencil, steal away, steal a minute of your time,
and best of all steal signs—steal home base!
If we had thyme, we'd go on to the *T*'s or to the *W*'s to see
if the phone would *wring*. Can you imagine exploring
without words to tell? That would be a kind of hell.
Lindsey said it's only paper that weighs something.
Thank goodness, I say, else our heads—and Ben's
new dictionary—would be as big as China.

Like A Child

Words school up like fish
On the playgrounds of our minds.
Faithful to patience we wait,
pencils poised, as if to think
our way into creation. But—
writing is the art of the moving hand,
wrote the poet Czeslaw Milosz.
So we must scribble deep
in quarries of the unimagined,
just like the hands that hammered
Aphrodite out of stone.

That War!

It's the children—
small, bundled, held
close against the cold,
bewildered, wide-eyed
torn from lives they are
just getting to know,
unaware they bear witness.
Not yet sacrificial lambs—
more like wildflowers
sown in the wind.

The Gift of Darkness

If you walk after midnight along
a South Florida beach in a certain
season, you might see a turtle as big
as your desk drift in on the waves.
Turn off your flashlight and be still.
She'll have come from far icy waters
to lay 100 or more eggs in this ancient
shoreline humans honor seasonally with
a lights-out gift of darkness. She'll
come ashore, crawl above the high tide
mark, and with back flippers dig three
feet, lay 100 or more eggs, nudge sand
over them, crawl back into the ocean
and swim away to colder, deeper waters.
Weeks later in pre-dawn hours, if lucky
you'll see hatchlings dig out and scramble
fast as their tiny legs will go for the light
that led their mother—the gleam of stars
and moon in waves. Against all odds
they'll swim 600 miles through whale-
and-shark-infested waters to reach
earth's one nutrient-rich floating nursery—
that deep blue, shoreless Sargasso Sea.

Big Bang

seems a comic book title
for such an ever evolving
unfathomable reality. Our
spitball Earth has spun 'round
for what seems like forever
while we—in the grip of our
seven-day creation story—
seldom seem to consider that
our Sun neither sets nor rises
as it consumes its last centuries
of fuel, that we orbit a source
of light that—just as old
wood burns the swiftest—
offers no promise of eternity.

Poverty

In a savage grind, rat and squirrel
tumble onto dirt of the school's
once-grassy playground, battling
without heed of boys and a dad

playing baseball. They fight as if
to death over what—morsel of food?
Defense of nest or newborn?
Honor in battle? Blood flashes

in the spit and dust. The beasts howl
a piercing harmony until lesser fates
prevail—futility, exhaustion. Rat
retreats, squeezes his bulk down

a hole at a hedge root. Squirrel limps
across hard ground to a tree, climbs
slowly. The boys shrug, turn back
to cracked bat and threadbare baseball.

From that Montana Bluff

we shade our eyes and watch
a buffalo herd graze toward us
across the high flat plains.
We're standing on a cliff where
generations ago Indians
stampeded those beasts over
the edge in mass slaughters
for fresh meat and hides,
signifying a cruel reality—
life on Earth demands slaughter.

The Sunflower

Of all the flowering plants
we've had in yards over decades
we never planted sunflowers.
Seldom do we see them in our
neighborhood. Yet when we
arrived home in North Carolina
from the funeral of my wife's
mother Mary Ellen in Florida,
there at the leading edge of our
front yard flower bed stood
one towering bright sunflower.

Tiny Seashells

A memory of my mother, Margaret Hancock Lee

Tiny seashells heaped like pennies
in that delicate curve of beach
where my mother settled old bones
and gently sifted, her mind in
gravity's grasp. How tenderly she
focused on remains so randomly
arrayed. *Oh pooh!* she replied when
I declared them merely unclaimed
freight of the tides. All these years,
and now I believe those shells were
Heaven's foothills in her eyes.

After Hours in the Gallery of Poems

After a reading by poet Jane Hirschfield

Go ahead, *take one*—
hanging here like
a painting on a paper
wall. Or *take them all*!
No harm befalls
any writer's heart.

That Deacon's Joke Still Thrills Me

I was a small boy then, but I still
vividly recall rushing back home
to see the new hardwood floors being
installed in the parsonage. As I entered
the living room, a deacon was on
his knees in the dining room, staring
at a board as he declared to my father,
> *Brother Lee, I cut this board*
> *three times and it's still too short!*

Life's Sweetest Mystery

for Mary Carol

and by far the most tender
is the freedom earned
by the heart's surrender.

Benediction

In memory of Clarence Jordan, Plezy Nelson and Jack Singletary

Come sunrise, we gather for a few words,
sing *Amazing Grace*, then walk the path
along the cornfield past the faded red
book-lined shack where the sudden death
occurred just the morning before. On up
along a lightly wooded slope, we see it,
neat as a campsite—a fresh grave, deep
and square-cornered. We never see
the men who through the night dug that grave
by lantern light—Plezy, a black laborer on
the farm, and Jack, the only white farmer-friend
of the deceased. But the tools of their labor
greet us—two shovels upright in the soil
like the sweaty remains of their own prayers.

* *Clarence Jordan, a scholar with a PhD in New Testament Greek, established Koinonia Farm near Americus, GA, in 1942 as a pre-Civil Rights-era experiment in Christian communal living based on New Testament accounts of the disciples' response to the crucifixion of Jesus. He also wrote and produced the Cotton Patch translation of the New Testament. Koinonia welcomed former sharecroppers (mostly black families) to work Koinonia's fields for fair wages and share a communal lunch every day. Koinonia bought an old bus to pick up rural black children and deliver them to their segregated schools. These activities sparked violence and aroused the Ku Klux Klan. When the lawyer Millard Fuller joined the enterprise, the community began building affordable houses for desperately poor families, efforts that evolved quickly into Habitat for Humanity.*

Notes

I'm especially grateful to my writer-editor wife Mary Carol for her close readings, and to poet-friends who have taught and shared poetry with me over the years—especially the poet/novelist Dannye Romine Powell of Charlotte, and the poet Thomas Lux of Atlanta, who was a co-founder of the long-running annual Palm Beach Poetry Festival.

Also, my three sisters, who were at the heart of the joyful home I was born into—Lina Ruth DiFiore, Margaret Grace Vaughan, and Mary Virginia Reedy. They enriched my life in so many adventurous ways, especially with brothers-in-law and 11 nephews and nieces. I was an uncle by age 7.

My parents, and Mary Carol's—Dallas Powell and Margaret Hancock Lee, and Walter Boone and Mary Ellen Lucas.

Our sons, Robert McInteer Lee, Dallas Paul Lee, and Christopher Sean Burdette; and their children—Dallas Daniel & Dillon Robert Lee; Elsa Gesina & Evan Johannes Lee; and Dallas Scout Burdette.

And of course, the teachers and editors who taught and encouraged me in a journalism career—David McHam and Dave Cheavens of Baylor University, Lew Williams of The Waco News-Tribune, Ron Autry of The Associated Press, and especially my dear friend Walker Knight of the Baptist Home Mission Board. Walker revolutionized church-based journalism by focusing on the urgent lives of the poorest and most neglected Americans among us.

Dallas McInteer Lee
Charlotte NC

www.ingramcontent.com/pod-product-compliance
Lightning Source LLC
Chambersburg PA
CBHW061257040426
42444CB00010B/2409